Greatest Motivational Quotes of All time

"When everything seems to be going against you, remember that the airplane takes off against the wind, not with it." – Henry Ford

"Your time is limited, don't waste it living someone else's life." – Steve Jobs

"Aim for the moon. If you miss, you may hit a star." – W. Clement

Nelson Mandela – Winston Churchill – Ghandi – Albert Einstein – Henry Ford –   Bob Marley – Charles Darwin – Benjamin Franklin – Thomas Jefferson

And More

Daniel Bulmez

DEDICATION

I dedicate this book to you, for blessing these pages with your beautiful gaze, and for giving your time to experience and share in this timeless wisdom. I hope you achieve your dreams and reach levels you never thought possible in all areas important to you.

Life is a beautiful journey, and it is made that much more beautiful when we play, work, and grow together.

CONTENTS

ACKNOWLEDGMENTS

I would like to thank my Mother and Father for always believing in me. Supporting me through the hardest times and with the little that they had. Thank you for doing the best that you could and knew how.

I would like to thank my amazing friends from whom I learnt so very much. I will always remember you for your support and for the things you may not even know you have given me, by being such amazing people who I can look up to and spend precious moments with.

You know who you are.

PREFACE

Introduction

Are you prepared to give up on your dreams and let others tell you what you can and cannot have? What you can and cannot do? What you can and cannot say? Or do you want to achieve success, overcome fear and live the life you want?

If you want the latter, then this book is for you.

These eternal quotes from the greatest minds in history have been selected to support you on your journey of building the life of your dreams, whatever that may look like. They can help build confidence and be by your side in times when things seem like they are overwhelming and life is not going your way. They are also here for when you have achieved part of your goals and you know that there is more to come, that the sky is the limit.

I sincerely wish you success and happiness so that you can be fulfilled and be loved by those around you.

Good luck on your journey and may all your best wishes come true.

How to use this book

This book contains 3 chapters which are important for achieving your dreams and success:

1. Overcoming Adversity
2. Pursuing Your Dreams
3. Perseverance and Determination

They are meant as a reference point for every time you feel you need inspiration and encouragement, to get you through challenging times so you may overcome them.

The worlds brightest minds of all time will be there next to you to encourage and support you through life's most challenging moments.

CHAPTER 1:

OVERCOMING ADVERSITY

Quotes about resilience, overcoming challenges, and finding strength in tough times to come out victorious.

1. "When everything seems to be going against you, remember that the airplane takes off against the wind, not with it." – Henry Ford

2. "Tough times never last, but tough people do." – Robert H. Schuller

3. "The phoenix must burn to emerge." – Janet Fitch

4. "When you come out of the storm, you won't be the same person who walked in. That's what the storm is all about." – Haruki Murakami

5. "Do not judge me by my success, judge me by how many times I fell down and got back up again." – Nelson Mandela

6. "It's not whether you get knocked down, it's whether you get up." – Vince Lombardi

7. "A river cuts through rock, not because of its power, but because of its persistence." – Jim Watkins

8. "You never know how strong you are until being strong is the only choice you have." – Bob Marley

9. "Problems are not stop signs, they are guidelines." – Robert H. Schuller

10. "When we are no longer able to change a situation, we are challenged to change ourselves." – Viktor E. Frankl

11. "It is not the strongest of the species that survive, nor the most intelligent, but the one most responsive to change." – Charles Darwin

12. "The greatest glory in living lies not in never falling, but in rising every time we fall." – Nelson Mandela

13.   "Rock bottom became the solid foundation on which I rebuilt my life." – J.K. Rowling

14.   "You may have to fight a battle more than once to win it." – Margaret Thatcher

15.   "You gain strength, courage, and confidence by every experience in which you really stop to look fear in the face." – Eleanor Roosevelt

16.   "A hero is an ordinary individual who finds the strength to persevere and endure in spite of

overwhelming obstacles." – Christopher Reeve

17. Out of suffering have emerged the strongest souls; the most massive characters are seared with scars." – Khalil Gibran

18. "I can be changed by what happens to me. But I refuse to be reduced by it." – Maya Angelou

19. "He who conquers himself is the mightiest warrior." – Confucius

20. "You have power over your mind – not outside events. Realize this, and you will find strength." – Marcus Aurelius

21. "Strength does not come from physical capacity. It comes from an indomitable will." – Mahatma Gandhi

22. "The best way out is always through." – Robert Frost

23. "The gem cannot be polished without friction, nor man perfected without trials." – Chinese Proverb

24.   "Life doesn't get easier or more forgiving, we get stronger and more resilient." – Steve Maraboli

25.   "The human capacity for burden is like bamboo – far more flexible than you'd ever believe at first glance." – Jodi Picoult

26.   "Our greatest glory is not in never falling, but in rising every time we fall." – Confucius

27.   "Although the world is full of suffering, it is full also of the overcoming of it." – Helen Keller

28.   "What lies behind us and what lies before us are tiny matters compared to what lies within us." – Ralph Waldo Emerson

29.   "Fall seven times, stand up eight." – Japanese Proverb

30.   "Turn your wounds into wisdom." – Oprah Winfrey

31.   "Success is not final, failure is not fatal: It is the courage to continue that counts." – Winston S. Churchill

32.   "It is during our darkest moments that we must focus to see the light." – Aristotle Onassis

33.   "Resilience is knowing that you are the only one that has the power and the responsibility to pick yourself up." – Mary Holloway

34.   "Pain is inevitable. Suffering is optional." – Haruki Murakami

35.   "Courage doesn't always roar. Sometimes courage is the little voice at the end of the day that says

I'll try again tomorrow." – Mary Anne Radmacher

36. "We must accept finite disappointment, but never lose infinite hope." – Martin Luther King Jr.

37. "In the middle of difficulty lies opportunity." – Albert Einstein

38. "The only way to make sense out of change is to plunge into it, move with it, and join the dance." – Alan Watts

39. "The human spirit is stronger than anything that

can happen to it." – C.C. Scott

40. "Challenges are what make life interesting and overcoming them is what makes life meaningful." – Joshua J. Marine

41. "Sometimes you don't realize your own strength until you come face to face with your greatest weakness." – Susan Gale

42. "Strength and growth come only through continuous effort and struggle." – Napoleon Hill

43.   "The greatest test of courage on earth is to bear defeat without losing heart." – R.G. Ingersoll

44.   "It's not the load that breaks you down, it's the way you carry it." – Lena Horne

45.   "You have to fight through some bad days to earn the best days of your life." – Unknown

46.   "Adversity has the effect of eliciting talents, which in prosperous circumstances would have lain dormant." – Horace

47. "There is no education like adversity." – Benjamin Disraeli

48. "Resilience is not about being able to bounce back like nothing has happened. It's about growing from the experience." – Unknown

49. "What does not kill me makes me stronger." – Friedrich Nietzsche

50. "Mountains do not rise without earthquakes." – Katherine Paterson

51.   "Life shrinks or expands in proportion to one's courage." – Anais Nin

52.   "It does not matter how slowly you go as long as you do not stop." – Confucius

53.   "The most effective way to do it, is to do it." – Amelia Earhart

54.   "Our greatest weakness lies in giving up. The most certain way to succeed is always to try just one more time." – Thomas A. Edison

55.　"I am not afraid of storms, for I am learning how to sail my ship." – Louisa May Alcott

56.　"The best revenge is massive success." – Frank Sinatra

57.　"It's not the strength of the body that counts, but the strength of the spirit." – J.R.R. Tolkien

58.　"I am thankful for my struggle because without it, I wouldn't have stumbled across my strength." – Alex Elle

59.   "Courage is resistance to fear, mastery of fear, not absence of fear." – Mark Twain

60.   "When you're finished changing, you're finished." – Benjamin Franklin

61.   "The biggest risk is not taking any risk... In a world that is changing really quickly, the only strategy that is guaranteed to fail is not taking risks." – Mark Zuckerberg

62.   "You can have it all. Just not all at once." – Oprah Winfrey

63. "Don't count the days; make the days count." – Muhammad Ali

64. "Strength does not come from winning. Your struggles develop your strengths." – Arnold Schwarzenegger

65. "If you never want to be criticized, for goodness' sake don't do anything new." – Jeff Bezos

66. "I love those who can smile in trouble." – Leonardo da Vinci

67. "No person will make a great business who

wants to do it all himself or get all the credit." – Andrew Carnegie

68.   "Obstacles don't have to stop you. If you run into a wall, don't turn around and give up. Figure out how to climb it, go through it, or work around it." – Michael Jordan

69.   "A woman is like a tea bag – you never know how strong she is until she gets in hot water." – Eleanor Roosevelt

70.   "I do not think that there is any other quality so essential to success of any

kind as the quality of perseverance." – John D. Rockefeller

71.   "It's fine to celebrate success, but it is more important to heed the lessons of failure." – Bill Gates

72.   "You only have to do a very few things right in your life so long as you don't do too many things wrong." – Warren Buffett

73.   "Your work is going to fill a large part of your life, and the only way to be truly satisfied is to do what you believe is great work." – Steve Jobs

74.   "You don't learn to walk by following rules. You learn by doing, and by falling over." – Richard Branson

75.   "However difficult life may seem, there is always something you can do and succeed at." – Stephen Hawking

76.   "Failure is simply the opportunity to begin again, this time more intelligently." – Henry Ford

77.   "You may encounter many defeats, but you must not be defeated." – Maya Angelou

78.   "All the adversity I've had in my life, all my troubles and obstacles, have strengthened me." – Walt Disney

79.   "A diamond is a chunk of coal that did well under pressure." – Henry Kissinger

80.   "The human spirit is to grow strong by conflict." – William Ellery Channing

81.   "Adversity causes some men to break; others to break records." – William Arthur Ward

82. "The only thing that overcomes hard luck is hard work." – Harry Golden

CHAPTER 2:

PURSUING YOUR DREAMS

Inspirational words on following your dreams, ambitions, and goals to achieve the life you deserve.

1. "Your time is limited, don't waste it living someone else's life." – Steve Jobs

2. "The future belongs to those who believe in the beauty of their dreams." – Eleanor Roosevelt

3. "Dream big and dare to fail." – Norman Vaughan

4. "You are never too old to set another goal or to dream a new dream." – C.S. Lewis

5. "I have learned that to be with those I like is enough." – Walt Whitman

6. "The only thing that will stop you from fulfilling your dreams is you." – Tom Bradley

7. "Whatever you can do, or dream you can, begin it. Boldness has genius, power, and magic in it." – Johann Wolfgang von Goethe

8. "Aim for the moon. If you miss, you may hit a star." – W. Clement Stone

9. "Setting goals is the first step in turning the invisible into the visible." – Tony Robbins

10.   "The only limit to our realization of tomorrow will be our doubts of today." – Franklin D. Roosevelt

11.   "What you get by achieving your goals is not as important as what you become by achieving your goals." – Henry David Thoreau

12.   "Do not follow where the path may lead. Go instead where there is no path and leave a trail." – Ralph Waldo Emerson

13.   "The best way to predict your future is to create it." – Abraham Lincoln

GREATEST MOTIVATIONAL QUOTES OF ALL TIME

14.   "To accomplish great things, we must not only act but also dream, not only plan but also believe." – Anatole France

15.   "All our dreams can come true, if we have the courage to pursue them." – Walt Disney

16.   "Success is not the key to happiness. Happiness is the key to success. If you love what you are doing, you will be successful." – Albert Schweitzer

17.   "I can't change the direction of the wind, but I can adjust my sails to always

reach my destination." –
Jimmy Dean

18.   "Keep your dreams alive. Understand to achieve anything requires faith and belief in yourself, vision, hard work, determination, and dedication." – Gail Devers

19.   "The only way to achieve the impossible is to believe it is possible." – Charles Kingsleigh

20.   "You have to dream before your dreams can come true." – A. P. J. Abdul Kalam

21.   "Believe you can and you're halfway there." – Theodore Roosevelt

22.   "Your goal should be just out of reach, but not out of sight." – Denis Waitley and Remi Witt

23.   "One way to keep momentum going is to have constantly greater goals." – Michael Korda

24.   "Life is short, fragile and does not wait for anyone. There will NEVER be a perfect time to pursue your dreams and goals." – Unknown

25.   "I'd rather regret the things I've done than regret the things I haven't done." – Lucille Ball

26.   "The only thing worse than starting something and failing ... is not starting something." – Seth Godin

27.   "Don't watch the clock; do what it does. Keep going." – Sam Levenson

28.   "You can't help everyone, but everyone can help someone." – Ronald Reagan

29.   "Determination is nothing without dedication and hard work." – Eshraq Jiad

30.   "The best dreams happen when you're awake." – Cherie Gilderbloom

31.   "If you want something you've never had, you must be willing to do something you've never done." – Thomas Jefferson

32.   "Don't be pushed by your problems; be led by your dreams." – Ralph Waldo Emerson

33.   "The only thing standing between you and your goal is the story you keep telling yourself as to why you can't achieve it." – Jordan Belfort

34.   "Dreams are not what you see in sleep, they are the things that don't let you sleep." – A.P.J. Abdul Kalam

35.   "Go confidently in the direction of your dreams. Live the life you've imagined." – Henry David Thoreau

36.   "Do not wait; the time will never be 'just right.'

Start where you stand, and work with whatever tools you may have at your command, and better tools will be found as you go along." – George Herbert

37.   "A year from now you may wish you had started today." – Karen Lamb

38.   "Act as if what you do makes a difference. It does." – William James

39.   "The future depends on what you do today." – Mahatma Gandhi

40.   "The distance between insanity and genius

is measured only by success."
– Bruce Feirstein

41.   "The only place
where dreams are impossible
is in your own mind." –
Emalie

42.   "Whatever the mind
can conceive and believe, it
can achieve." – Napoleon
Hill

43.   "You can't use up
creativity. The more you use,
the more you have." – Maya
Angelou

44.   "The harder the
battle, the sweeter the
victory." – Les Brown

45.   "Opportunities don't happen. You create them." – Chris Grosser

46.   "Do one thing every day that scares you." – Eleanor Roosevelt

47.   "Your life does not get better by chance, it gets better by change." – Jim Rohn

48.   "I am always doing that which I cannot do, in order that I may learn how to do it." – Pablo Picasso

49.   "Success usually comes to those who are too

busy to be looking for it." –
Henry David Thoreau

50.   "The way to get
started is to quit talking and
begin doing." – Walt Disney

51.   "There is only one
thing that makes a dream
impossible to achieve: the
fear of failure." – Paulo
Coelho

52.   "You miss 100% of
the shots you don't take." –
Wayne Gretzky

53.   "I never dreamed
about success, I worked for
it." – Estée Lauder

54.   "Limitations live only in our minds. But if we use our imaginations, our possibilities become limitless." – Jamie Paolinetti

55.   "The only place where your dream becomes impossible is in your own thinking." – Robert H Schuller

56.   "The biggest adventure you can take is to live the life of your dreams." – Oprah Winfrey

57.   "Everything you've ever wanted is on the other side of fear." – George Addair

58. "Believe in yourself. You are braver than you think, more talented than you know, and capable of more than you imagine." – Roy T. Bennett

59. "It often requires more courage to dare to do right than to fear to do wrong." – Abraham Lincoln

60. "Your work is to discover your work and then with all your heart to give yourself to it." – Buddha

61. "The man who has no imagination has no wings." – Muhammad Ali

62.   "Life takes on meaning when you become motivated, set goals and charge after them in an unstoppable manner." – Les Brown

63.   "If you set your goals ridiculously high and it's a failure, you will fail above everyone else's success." – James Cameron

64.   "I'd rather attempt to do something great and fail than to attempt to do nothing and succeed." – Robert H. Schuller

65.   "The secret of getting ahead is getting started." – Mark Twain

66.   "Develop success from failures. Discouragement and failure are two of the surest stepping stones to success." – Dale Carnegie

67.   "Imagination is more important than knowledge. Knowledge is limited. Imagination encircles the world." – Albert Einstein

68.   "You become what you believe." – Oprah Winfrey

69.   "He who is not courageous enough to take risks will accomplish nothing in life." – Muhammad Ali

70.   "The mind is the limit. As long as the mind can envision the fact that you can do something, you can do it." – Arnold Schwarzenegger

71.   "One of the only ways to get out of a tight box is to invent your way out." – Jeff Bezos

72.   "When something is important enough, you do it even if the odds are not in your favor." – Elon Musk

73.   "I have been impressed with the urgency of doing. Knowing is not enough; we must apply. Being willing is not enough; we must do." – Leonardo da Vinci

74.   "If you want to be happy, set a goal that commands your thoughts, liberates your energy, and inspires your hopes." – Andrew Carnegie

75.   "I can accept failure, everyone fails at something. But I can't accept not trying." – Michael Jordan

76.   "Don't be afraid to give up the good to go for the great." – John D. Rockefeller

77.   "Your most unhappy customers are your greatest source of learning." – Bill Gates

78.   "It takes 20 years to build a reputation and five minutes to ruin it. If you think about that, you'll do things differently." – Warren Buffett

79.   "However difficult life may seem, there is always something you can do and

succeed at." – Stephen Hawking

80.   "Anything's possible if you've got enough nerve." – J.K. Rowling

81.   "You will face many defeats in life, but never let yourself be defeated." – Maya Angelou

82.   "All our dreams can come true, if we have the courage to pursue them." – Walt Disney

CHAPTER 3:

PERSEVERANCE AND DETERMINATION

Quotes about the power of persistence, hard work, and never giving up so you can overcome the hardest life challenges.

1. "Energy and persistence conquer all things." – Benjamin Franklin

2. "Success is the sum of small efforts, repeated day in and day out." – Robert Collier

3. "Perseverance is not a long race; it is many short races one after the other." – Walter Elliot

4. "Our greatest weakness lies in giving up. The most certain way to succeed is always to try just one more time." – Thomas Edison

5. "Hard work beats talent when talent doesn't work hard." – Tim Notke

6. "The only place where success comes before work is in the dictionary." – Vidal Sassoon

7. "I'm a greater believer in luck, and I find the harder I work the more I have of it." – Thomas Jefferson

8. "Through hard work, perseverance and a faith in God, you can live your dreams." – Ben Carson

9. "Success is no accident. It is hard work, perseverance,

learning, studying, sacrifice and most of all, love of what you are doing or learning to do." – Pelé

10. "Perseverance is the hard work you do after you get tired of doing the hard work you already did." – Newt Gingrich

11. "The difference between a successful person and others is not a lack of strength, not a lack of knowledge, but rather a lack in will." – Vince Lombardi

12. "A dream doesn't become reality through magic; it takes sweat,

determination, and hard work." – Colin Powell

13.   "With the new day comes new strength and new thoughts." – Eleanor Roosevelt

14.   "Persistence can change failure into extraordinary achievement." – Marv Levy

15.   "The road to success is dotted with many tempting parking spaces." – Will Rogers

16.   "Opportunities are usually disguised as hard work, so most people don't

recognize them." – Ann
Landers

17.   "There is no
substitute for hard work." –
Thomas Edison

18.   "Perseverance is
failing 19 times and
succeeding the 20th." – Julie
Andrews

19.   "What you do today
can improve all your
tomorrows." – Ralph
Marston

20.   "Success is the result
of perfection, hard work,
learning from failure, loyalty,

and persistence." – Colin Powell

21.   "Continuous effort — not strength or intelligence — is the key to unlocking our potential." – Winston Churchill

22.   "The harder you work for something, the greater you'll feel when you achieve it." – Unknown

23.   "Talent is cheaper than table salt. What separates the talented individual from the successful one is a lot of hard work." – Stephen King

24.　"Success is walking from failure to failure with no loss of enthusiasm." – Winston Churchill

25.　"Never give up, for that is just the place and time that the tide will turn." – Harriet Beecher Stowe

26.　"Great works are performed not by strength but by perseverance." – Samuel Johnson

27.　"The three great essentials to achieve anything worthwhile are, first, hard work; second, stick-to-itiveness; third, common sense." – Thomas A. Edison

28.   "Patience, persistence and perspiration make an unbeatable combination for success." – Napoleon Hill

29.   "Perseverance is the secret of all triumphs." – Victor Hugo

30.   "If you are going through hell, keep going." – Winston Churchill

31.   "Success seems to be largely a matter of hanging on after others have let go." – William Feather

32.   "The only failure is not to try." – George Clooney

33.   "The harder the conflict, the more glorious the triumph." – Thomas Paine

34.   "It does not matter how slowly you go, as long as you do not stop." – Confucius

35.   "I am not discouraged, because every wrong attempt discarded is another step forward." – Thomas Edison

36.   "Don't wish it were easier. Wish you were better."
– Jim Rohn

37.   "The world is full of magical things patiently waiting for our wits to grow sharper." – Bertrand Russell

38.   "When you get to the end of your rope, tie a knot and hang on." – Franklin D. Roosevelt

39.   "Many of life's failures are people who did not realize how close they were to success when they gave up." – Thomas A. Edison

40.   "Diligence is the mother of good fortune." – Benjamin Disraeli

41.   "You just can't beat the person who never gives up." – Babe Ruth

42.   "Effort only fully releases its reward after a person refuses to quit." – Napoleon Hill

43.   "Success is the result of hard work, learning from failure, loyalty, and persistence." – Colin Powell

44.   "I find that the harder I work, the more luck

I seem to have." – Thomas Jefferson

45.   "Perseverance is a great element of success. If you only knock long enough and loud enough at the gate, you are sure to wake up somebody." – Henry Wadsworth Longfellow

46.   "The difference between try and triumph is just a little umph!" – Marvin Phillips

47.   "Little strokes fell great oaks." – Benjamin Franklin

48.   "Keep your dreams alive. Understand to achieve anything requires faith and belief in yourself, vision, hard work, determination, and dedication." – Gail Devers

49.   "The difference between the impossible and the possible lies in a person's determination." – Tommy Lasorda

50.   "The future belongs to those who believe in the beauty of their dreams." – Eleanor Roosevelt

51.   "I hated every minute of training, but I said, 'Don't quit. Suffer now and

live the rest of your life as a champion.'" – Muhammad Ali

52.   "It's not whether you get knocked down, it's whether you get up." – Vince Lombardi

53.   "The most certain way to succeed is always to try just one more time." – Thomas Edison

54.   "You have to fight to reach your dream. You have to sacrifice and work hard for it." – Lionel Messi

55.   "Most of the important things in the world

have been accomplished by people who have kept on trying when there seemed to be no hope at all." – Dale Carnegie

56.   "Don't judge each day by the harvest you reap but by the seeds that you plant." – Robert Louis Stevenson

57.   "The road to success and the road to failure are almost exactly the same." – Colin R. Davis

58.   "Success is not the key to happiness. Happiness is the key to success. If you love what you are doing, you

will be successful." – Albert Schweitzer

59.　"Our greatest fear should not be of failure but of succeeding at things in life that don't really matter." – Francis Chan

60.　"The only real mistake is the one from which we learn nothing." – Henry Ford

61.　"Go for it now. The future is promised to no one." – Wayne Dyer

62.　"Hard work spotlights the character of people: some turn up their sleeves, some turn up their noses, and some don't turn up at all." – Sam Ewing

63.   "I've missed more than 9000 shots in my career. I've lost almost 300 games. 26 times, I've been trusted to take the game-winning shot and missed. I've failed over and over and over again in my life. And that is why I succeed." – Michael Jordan

64.   "The secret of getting ahead is getting started." – Mark Twain

65.   "It's not that I'm so smart, it's just that I stay with

problems longer." – Albert
Einstein

66.   "Do what you have
to do until you can do what
you want to do." – Oprah
Winfrey

67.   "I knew that if I
failed I wouldn't regret that,
but I knew the one thing I
might regret is not trying." –
Jeff Bezos

68.   "It had long since
come to my attention that
people of accomplishment
rarely sat back and let things
happen to them. They went
out and happened to things."
– Leonardo da Vinci

69. "People who are unable to motivate themselves must be content with mediocrity, no matter how impressive their other talents." – Andrew Carnegie

70. "I've failed over and over and over again in my life. And that is why I succeed." – Michael Jordan

71. "You must do the thing you think you cannot do." – Eleanor Roosevelt

72.　"I'm convinced that about half of what separates the successful entrepreneurs from the non-successful ones is pure perseverance." – Steve Jobs

73.　"Do not be embarrassed by your failures, learn from them and start again." – Richard Branson

74.　"Whether you think you can, or you think you can't – you're right." – Henry Ford

75.　"I have not failed. I've just found 10,000 ways that won't work." – Thomas Edison

76.   " All our dreams can come true, if we have the courage to pursue them." – Walt Disney

77.   "It always seems impossible until it's done." – Nelson Mandela

I hope you have enjoyed these timeless pieces of wisdom left by the greatest minds of all time. I wish that they instill confidence and belief in you. May they bring you motivation and success like you have never imagined before so that you may live the life you deserve.

I believe you have great power to achieve all of your dreams and that you are on the right path to achieve them.

Good luck on your journey my friend!

ABOUT THE AUTHOR

I remember it like I was yesterday. I was 7, living with my grandmother in the countryside in a little town of only 800 people, when my parents came and took me away on the greatest journey of my life. Living on 3 continents and in 5 countries, little did I know where life would take me decades later. Halfway across the word. Despite a lifetime of tirelessly educating myself and working in Private Equity in one of the most revered financial capitals of the world, little did I know that I would end up reaching the age of 37 having to begin all over again.

Finally learning that a life long of learning has just begun.
Humbled by the realization that I actually know very little.

Life is like that, one day you feel like you are on top of the world and the next you realize you have a lot to learn. Through the good times and the bad, I have learned that staying resilient and motivated is one of the most important things and there is no better way than learning from amazing people and through beautiful experiences. What more amazing people could we wish to learn from then from the greatest minds of all time who have changed the world as we know it and have blessed us with their teachings. Which they have generously left in their numerous texts. Gold mines scattered through history waiting for us to discover them.

These important lessons have changed the course of millions before us and they are now here to light out path to success.

Good luck on your journey dear friends, may you gain the success you seek and the happiness you deserve.

Daniel

Made in the USA
Coppell, TX
23 May 2024

32417319R00046